WHY AM I TELLING YOU THIS?

And Other Poems from Psychotherapy

Brad Sachs, Ph.D.

WHY AM I TELLING YOU THIS?

Editor: Clarinda Harriss
Graphic design: Ace Kieffer
Author photo: Fern Eisner

Cover art:
Hernan Bas, *Ennui (or, The Endless Conversation)*, 2013
Courtesy of the Artist and Paulson Bott Press

BrickHouse Books, Inc. 2015
306 Suffolk Road
Baltimore, MD 21218

Distributor: Itasca Books, Inc.

ISBN: 978-1-938144-30-1

Printed in the United States of America

INTRODUCTION

The poet's obligation is to be a voice for all those who have no voice
—**Pablo Neruda**

Having identified and envisioned myself as a poet long before I became a psychotherapist, I have always tried to listen for the poetry nesting in the province of my patients' tumbling narratives. In a way, it should not be a surprise that psychotherapy patients speak the language of poetry because poetry arises from much the same psychological state that therapy does. The therapeutic experience and the creative experience rely upon a similar loosening and softening of the boundaries between inner life and outer life, past and present, certainty and doubt, dream and awakening—both serve as bridges between what is revered and reviled, what is sought and abhorred, what is desired and discarded.

I do not take notes *during* clinical sessions, but I always reserve some time after each appointment to write up a page or two of comments. This documentation is generally comprised of a summary of the clinical content and personal matters that were attended to during that particular session, as well as a laying of the groundwork for the following sessions (concerns to address, questions to ask, assignments to follow up on, themes and hypotheses to pursue). However, I have always tried to conclude my note-taking by composing one poem—even a very short one—that, to me, captures an important facet of the patient's experience.

Sometimes, the poem that results is a simple, close-to-verbatim transcription of a fragment of the patient's actual words during an appointment. Sometimes, the poem is a short distillation of a much longer narrative that the patient had spilled out, pared down to (what is in my opinion) its elemental meaning. Sometimes, the poem is composed of words that the patient never actually spoke, but that I imagine s/he *wanted* to speak, and *would have* spoken had his/her internal editor or censor not interrupted the flow of feelings, shut the wires down, and buried the signal beneath thick layers of emotional batting. Sometimes the poem is a reduction, a written crystallization of what the patient was revealing to me, and/or to him/herself, throughout the course of several separate sessions, or perhaps even throughout the entire course of treatment itself.

When I first began the process of conceiving these poems, I held the belief that I was essentially playing a passive role, one that was somewhat akin to a ventriloquist's dummy, manipulated (albeit in the best sense of that word) into channeling or articulating the patient's truest, purest voice, the one that yearns to be spoken and that longs to be heard—and without there being any observable effort or authorship on my part. But in re-reading, re-visiting and re-experiencing them as I prepared this collection, and reflecting upon what I'd actually composed, the process began to seem more complicated than that, somewhat mysterious and elusive, not quite so easy to pin down.

Somehow, when the patient's inner world and my own inner world experienced a particular kind of encounter that was both observable and invisible, collision and embrace, mesh and clash, something important passed between us, and the poem—or at least the germ of the poem—until then lying silent and dormant, suddenly or gradually revealed itself. Somehow an intimate encounter with an Other stirred me to my depths, and a poem *insisted* that it be written, a therapeutic tale *demanded* to be told. Somehow the words that were regularly exchanged between my patient and I were alchemically condensed into literature, and it was as if the two of us had uncannily co-authored a chronicle that I transcribed, one that made us both feel more connected and more human, better able to sense a better way of being in the world.

Walt Whitman wrote, "I say the word or two that has to be said… and remind every man and woman of something," Regardless of how they arose—within *me*, within my *patient*, or, perhaps more accurately, within the sacred space created by and residing between the two of us—these poems in each instance represent a small vignette of the human predicament, one that reflects and refracts both the wondrous darkness and the difficult light that lies beneath all of us. It is for this reason that I have chosen to share them.

THE POETRY OF THERAPY, THE THERAPY OF POETRY

Sigmund Freud once commented, "Wherever I go, I find that a poet has already been." Surely, before psychotherapy ever existed, there was poetry, and the first individuals who ever became (or realized that they were innately) skilled at psychological treatment did so by mastering rhythm and meter, story and song, enchantment and incantation—those were (and to some extent remain) the most universal healing arts, the modalities that house the greatest of curative properties.

So although there are certainly differences between the practice of psychotherapy and the practice of poetry, it remains useful to consider carefully the ways in which they overlap and replicate each other.

Rita Dove avers, "The poet seeks not to ignore the shadow, but to describe it and the sun that created it." Poetry and psychotherapy both encourage journeys into one's self, seeking to create a home for both shadow and sun and inviting the complicated relationship between the two to be dramatized and expressed. They both serve to simultaneously de-mystify and re-mystify, to operate as conduits between what is clear and encrypted, what is congruent and contradictory, what is rational and magical, what is ancient and contemporary, what is real and not fully realized, what is known and unknowable.

The poetic and the psychotherapeutic narrative rely on ambiguity and ambivalence, leaving out as much as they say, connoting as much as they denote, suggesting as much as they declare, concealing as much as they reveal. To be most meaningful and profound, they depend on the holes in the story as much as they depend on the story itself, spiraling away from what is familiar and tidy, intently resisting the temptation to be fully solved or resolved, nailed down or understood.

To do their jobs well, the psychotherapist and the poet must both find a way to be present, to bear witness and pay tender attention to the depth and breadth of human experience. They must suspend disbelief, question assumptions, discard theories, disrupt complacency, elude the customary allegiance to superficial reality, and take the risk of peering nervously but surely into the vast abyss that lies just below our conscious thought and awareness. They must defend and pursue the sanctity of their vision, the guiding faith that awareness trumps tranquility, that discovery is more important than knowledge, that wonder is deeper than certainty, that the search for and the encounter with the unexamined and the inexplicable is more worthwhile than a complacent resignation to one's worldly existence. The psychotherapist and the poet feel compelled to listen to the inchoate murmurings of others, and of themselves, with a sensitivity that is typically uncalled for in the everyday world, so that they can pursue and privilege their healing powers. They must be hospitable to that which is most disturbing, most desperate, and most arresting about the human condition. As Anne Sexton wrote about her experience with psychiatric medications and hospitalizations: "My fans think I got well, but I didn't. I just became a poet."

The results of poetic and psychotherapeutic encounters are aligned, as well. In either case, we find ourselves suddenly seized and awakened, navigating previously unexplored territories, opening up to and pursuing different horizons, suddenly brisk and urgent with new ideas and renewed inspiration as we come in contact with something about ourselves that has always been vivid and essential, but that for too long—possibly forever—has been essentially overlooked. Poetry and psychotherapy are soul-forging, soul-feeding experiences that render us more whole, more complete, and more sufficient, that summon us to take the risk of falling more deeply in love with ourselves, with others, and with the world.

SO WHY DID I WRITE THESE POEMS?

I have woven a parachute out of everything broken.
—**William Stafford**

Since first undertaking the on-going endeavor of composing poetry as part of my clinical documentation, I have often asked myself this question and the most comprehensive answer I have been able to come up with is…I'm not absolutely sure. However, I do have some ideas as to what prompted me to begin taking notes, and "taking note", in poetic fashion.

My work as a therapist is rewarding work, and I feel blessed every day that I am able to do it, but gratifying as it may be, it is frightfully *hard* work. What makes it hard is that I am forced, like it or not, session after session, to confront the grim, impossible truths of the human condition—that our most precious dreams and desires will never be entirely fulfilled, that no one can ever rescue or protect us from anguish and loss, that we have entered and will depart the world alone, that there are limits to the powers of love, care, and kindness, that we will forever be held hostage by terrors and longings, appetites and regrets, over which we have distressingly little control, and that the world somehow existed before us and will go on without us.

Rare is the encounter with a patient when I don't feel a wrench deep in my chest—anything from loneliness to rage, from sorrow to wanting—and my heart becomes drenched, if not absolutely flooded, with an overflow of uncommandable feelings that seem to have no limit, no end.

Of course, it is my job—better, my *duty*—at these times not just to collapse in the face of this emotional intensity, or to desperately attempt to ward it off or shake loose from it. Instead I endeavor to welcome and explore it, to embark with the patient on a conjoint, steadfast search for the seeds of wholeness, wisdom, and redemption that lie, reluctantly but eagerly, beneath pain's forbidding surface, and to patiently nurture those seeds into fruition.

Somehow, the process of writing poetry based on the intimate conversation held in my office allows me to do this, and provides me with some solace, some protection, some buoyancy, and some resilience, as my patient and I tread blindly together through the unnavigable dark, attemping to rescue consciousness from oblivion and triumphantly hold it aloft. When despondency, defeat and despair have steadily bled themselves into our very bones and brazenly taken up residence in our threadbare souls, speaking up in the face of what feels unspeakable, uttering what feels unutterable, conceiving of what feels inconceivable, calms my spirit and seems to be my noblest response, the best way I can find to metabolize this experience without sinking into hopelessness, the best vantage point from which to view with empathy and compassion the emotional mysteries that lie at the heart of human motive, human conflict, human desire, indeed humanity itself.

So in literally "living to tell about it" and salvaging something authentic and poetic from the therapeutic encounter, I affirm both my own and my patients' capacity to live with, learn from and ultimately transcend suffering. If "words fail me", then, in essence, I am failing my patients. My giving voice to their wandery, plaintive laments enables the two of us to better harness the vast powers hidden therein, creating greater possibilities for healing and growth, and, in the process, enriching both of our lives.

Each poem, then, stands proudly as a small symbol of emotional triumph, creating a psychological beachhead that enables the patient and me to consolidate our position and dig in against the nefarious forces of purposelessness and meaninglessness. As the poet Robert Hayden eloquently states: "All art is pain/suffered and outlived."

I have come to realize that there are other motivations at work here, as well. The practice of writing a poem after each session forces me to listen with a different kind of ear to my patients' narratives, an ear that then becomes automatically attuned to different, less rational, logical facets of their experience. As a result, each patient is more likely to sound unique and distinct, even if the identified problem that has brought him/her to me for treatment is not significantly different from the identified problems of other patients. Once I'm able to capture patients' unique melodies, it makes me more interested in them, which in turn translates into their becoming more interested in themselves, an interest that always pays handsome dividends in the currency of the patient's self-awareness, self-discovery, and self-assuredness.

I have also slowly learned that writing poems about my patients allows something to take place that I was initially trained *not* to allow for, but that I have found to be of profound importance in the healing relationship, nonetheless—I am referring to the process of encouraging myself to let my patients *matter* to me, and insisting not only that they change as a result of *me*, but that I change as a result of *them*.

Most clinical training dictates that the patient be kept at a distance. The emphasis on learning to identify diagnostic categories and preparing standardized assessments and manualized treatments based on these categories can wind up serving the function of shrinking the patient, making her seem more object than subject, smaller and more confined rather than larger and more expansive. Much of my own training entailed being carefully instructed that the primary goal of treatment is to alter the patient in some way—to fix her, cure her, make her better, different, or improved—rather than to *be* altered. I was schooled to interpret stories, decipher meaning, and "administer" therapy as one might administer a shot, without any transformation taking place in the administrator.

It has taken me a long time to realize, however, that in devoting myself to doing the opposite, to in fact being changed by my patients, I paradoxically become a better agent of and catalyst for change in *their* lives. When patients know that their sagas of loss, love, struggle and survival matter to me—and patients always know if they matter to their therapist, whether their therapist is writing or sharing poems about them or not—then they are more likely to matter to themselves, which greatly increases the odds that they will marshal their inner resources and knowingly pursue growth and transformation.

So writing poetry about my patients prevents me from ever becoming too clinical, too jaded, too detached from my patients' pain, because once this happens, intended helpfulness becomes unhelpful, and what is supposed to be therapy becomes counter-therapeutic. Each poem is an acknowledgment of my respect for my patients' souls, a testament to my becoming heir to their heroic legacy, and I have no choice but to feel and to be different as a result of this rich inheritance.

Finally, I have frequently noticed that, in more widely casting my cognitive net and dipping into poetic waters after each hour, I am able to hone in on important issues and possibilities that I might have neglected or missed entirely during that hour. Many times I am surprised—even alarmed—by the poem that persistently pecks and pokes its way out of the eggshell of my consciousness to come alive on paper, especially when it initially appears to have little, or nothing at all, to do with the agenda that I had thought my patient and I were earnestly sponsoring and pursuing.

An offhanded observation on the part of the patient that actually held great significance, a "vibe" or feeling that one or both of us harbored but that neither of us called any attention to, an embryonic but stubborn intuition originating with the patient, myself, or both of us that was subtle but unmistakably present nonetheless—I have consistently harvested all of these, sometimes with chilling clarity, when I persuade my poetic instinct to sharpen its instrument, gently slide its way under the surface of the session, and investigate, with surgical precision, what Octavio Paz refers to as our "ever more ancient and naked states."

When I have led workshops for clinicians on bringing a more poetic voice to their therapeutic treatment, I am usually asked whether or not I ever share these poems with my patients. The answer is that I have not, even though there have been numerous times when I have been tempted to. My decision to keep these poems entirely to myself might appear to run counter to many of the motivations for undertaking this verse-making in the first place—after all, aren't I limiting its potential impact on the therapeutic encounter if I don't ever share these lyrics with my crucial co-author, the patient?

I have thought about this long and hard, and suppose that the main reason I have chosen not to is due to the potential hazards that exist. Any form of therapist self-disclosure runs the risk of distracting a patient from his/her own gleanings, explorations, and insights, and making the therapist more of a focus than the patient. As I have gradually discovered, these poems are not just about my patients, they are as much, if not more so, about *me,* and bringing them into the treatment conversation might unintentionally but unavoidably shift the spotlight away from him/her and onto me, a transaction that can quickly negate the power of the therapeutic relationship.

A "disclosure" of this sort might also create a certain self-consciousness that would impair the free flow of thoughts, ideas, and associations that is necessary for therapeutic work. I want my patients to be *less* concerned about what they're thinking and saying, not more concerned, and if they become too distracted by or alert to what I make of their words, it could hinder their spontaneity. They need to be asking, "Who am I?", "Why do I do what I do?", and "Who do I want to become?" rather than "I wonder if what I'm saying is going to turn into a poem?" or "Was this material not interesting enough for you to create poetry out of?"

But shared with the patient or not, I maintain the belief that the adventurous enterprise of poetry is one that not only augments and enhances the strength and efficacy of psychotherapy, but that ultimately unmasks hidden truths and helps us to understand more about, and come to terms with, what it means to be human. In sharing these poems—culled from the thousands that I've written—I am hopeful that the hard-earned revelations and illuminations that emerged from the courageous quests that my patients and I collaborated on bring perspective and direction to the striving for meaning and the voyaging of the spirit that every one of us is in eternal engagement with.

...a poetry as impure as old clothes, as a body with its foodstains and its shame, with wrinkles, observations, dreams, wakefulness, prophesies, declarations of love and hate, stupidities, shocks, idylls, negations, doubts, affirmations and taxes
—Pablo Neruda

A NOTE TO THE READER

I have arranged these poems such that the narrative sequence loosely resembles the chronological arc of human development. I have generally chosen to group together several or more poems that address a similar topic, so that the reader can encounter similar themes from different patients' perspectives.

Throughout the book, identifying details have been altered to protect the confidentiality of my patients. Any similarities to individuals living or dead are purely coincidental.

In the dark times
Will there also be singing?
Yes, there will be singing
About the dark times
—Bertolt Brecht

Tell me about despair, yours,
And I will tell you about mine.

From "Wild Geese", by Mary Oliver

FIRST SESSION

I will tell you this:
That I am really easy to piss off
That you better be careful with what you say
That I'm on my last nerve
That I'm not sure I can go on
That there will be days
When I will just sit here and cry
And cry
And cry
And you better let me cry
And you better not cry
And I will be angry with you
For not crying

HERE'S WHAT YOU SHOULD KNOW:

I complain about everything...
I complain about my kids
I complain about my job
I complain about my husband
I complain about my house
I complain about my neighborhood
I complain about the weather
I complain about the schools
I will now get to work figuring out
How to complain about you

DUMP

I've got nothing to talk about today.

> I should warn you, however,
> That I did take a dump in your bathroom
> And now I think the toilet might be clogged,
> You better check it when we're done in here
> I thought you should also know
> That your toilet paper is a little on the rough side
> All this money I'm paying you
> You really ought to invest in softer toilet paper
> My butt's *still* sore

That's about all I have to say today.

EVER

No smoking in here, eh?
I figured as much
Figured you'd be a clean liver
Look at you sitting there
All healthy
Clean clothes, clean lungs
Nothing dirty about you
Except your shoes,
They look a little shabby
But everything else
Rosy and clean-cut
Ever been in trouble?
Ever owed anybody money
And you didn't have a dime?
Ever sleep with a woman
Whose husband wanted to knife you?
Ever sat up all night
With a needle in your veins
And you still want it?
Ever screamed to God?
Just screamed your freaking lungs out
Yelling,
"God, God,
"Oh, God, Oh, God"?

RATTLED

Does *anything* rattle you?
I had a dream the other night that I sat here in your office
And started removing my shirt
Lifting it over my head
And your eyes grew big
And you came over
And buried your head in my breasts
And stroked my hair
And I held your head in my hands
And pressed it against me,
Saying, "*There, there...*"
And I woke up all wet
And now you're rattled,
Aren't you?

GETTING STARTED

No, I didn't write that letter to my father
No, I didn't make it to the gym
No, I didn't practice those breathing exercises that you showed me
I didn't do any of the things you asked me to do
That I **agreed** to do
All I did was sit around
And realize that
I wasn't doing anything
What can I say?
I'm an asshole.

JUST TELL ME

One of my twins is dying
The other is alive
In another week, my doctor says,
I'll be carrying one dead baby inside of me
And one living one
She tells me if I keep the dead one inside me
Another few weeks
Then the living one has a better chance of being born healthy
But if they go right in and get the dead one out
As soon as it dies
The living one may be born too early,
Possibly with problems,
Now tell me what I'm supposed to do here,
Will you?
Just tell me…

WHAT IT WAS

I was afraid of the silence
I was afraid of the night
I was afraid of the stars and the moon
So I did what needed to be done
I finally did it
I cannot tell you what I did
Although I know that you want to know
But I can tell you that
Whenever I look at the sky,
I think about it
But I will not tell you
What it was
You can't make me tell you
What it was
Can you?

HAVE I TOLD YOU ABOUT THE TIME

My father came into my bedroom
And did all sorts of terrible things to me
And then did the same terrible things
To my sister
While I watched, helpless?
And then he left
And we both hugged each other
Rocked ourselves to sleep, sobbing…
This really is not my story
I just wanted a chance to tell it
I just wanted you to hear it

GRIEF

I'm here because
My husband is not
Hit by a bus
Last month
Can you believe it?
If you can believe it,
I'm out of here
If you can't,
I'll return

LAST

I saw you leave the office the last time I was here
I was fiddling with some stuff in my car
In the parking lot after we were done
And looked up to see you
Locking up the office
Getting into your car
Driving off
You seemed so lonely

DAMN

When I was young
I was **so** beautiful
You would have fallen in love with me in an instant
You and everyone else
You wouldn't be sitting across from me
You'd be following me from club to café
Wishing you could dance with me
You and every other fellah
You would never be able to sit still in my presence
You'd give anything to dance with me
To feel my arms around your neck
To smell my long, soft hair
You're not going to be able to make me young again, are you?
Damn you

MAD

It wasn't so long ago
I drove the boys mad
Just by showing a little skin here and there
An extra button unbuttoned on my blouse
The sleeves of my sweater pulled up
Crossing my legs in a skirt
Oh, I could *feel* their temperatures rising!
Now, I feel like I could undress
In the middle of the street
In the middle of the day
And nothing would happen
Traffic wouldn't stop
Cars wouldn't honk
Life would go on around me
I'd stand there naked,
Ignored,
Makes *me* mad

HERE'S WHY I'M HERE

Because a student of mine stayed after school
To get help with Calculus
And as she sat next to me at my desk
She put her hand on my thigh
And left it there
I got hard instantly
But she never moved her hand
And I didn't move her hand
I didn't dare touch her hand
We finished up and she left
And now all day
Every day
All I feel
Is her hand

I'M HERE TO FIGURE OUT

Why the wrong man's kisses
Always feel so right
Why his hands
Always feel so warm
Why his hugs
Always feel so strong
Why his love
Always feels so good

WHY AM I TELLING YOU THIS?

Stuck at home all weekend after that blizzard
My kids were driving me crazy, fought the whole time,
My husband didn't want to do anything
Except watch poker on TV
I made brownies, batch after batch,
Ate more than all the kids combined
Must've gained 5 pounds in 2 days
Feel like a whale, now,
Like a beached whale…
　　　　Why am I telling you this?
　　　　You don't care,
　　　　You just go home,
　　　　Cash my check
　　　　Fuck your wife
　　　　Play with your perfect kids
　　　　Not a goddamn care in the world
　　　　You don't have a goddamn care in the world,
　　　　Do you?

BRIDGE

I decided it was
Finally time to kill myself
Thought I'd jump off
The Chesapeake Bay Bridge
Hitch-hiked a ride
But to avoid suspicion
Asked to be let out
At the Amoco
Near the base
And there I saw
A tobacco shack:
Half-price smokes!
So I bought a carton
Stood there in the moonlight
Staring at the bridge
Smoking 'till my lungs burned
Now
Go break some psychological shit
Out of *that* one,
Doc

EASY ON EVERYONE

I already know how I'll kill myself
I'll undress,
Lie down in the bathtub
Turn the water on nice and warm
Fill it up, shut the water,
Smoke a cigar, down a whiskey,
Put a revolver in my mouth
And eat a bullet
That way, there'll be no clean-up
It'll be easy on everyone
Just drain the tub and pull me out
I always try to make things
Easy on everyone

NIGHT GARDEN

You asked me to come up with a hobby
I think I'm going to start a night garden
I'll wait until my wife and the kids are asleep
And I'll go out and plant things under the moon
And they'll blossom in the dark
It'll be quiet, so quiet,
And peaceful, so peaceful
Just me and the moon, man
Just me and the moon

HATE

There's this place inside of me
Where I go to do all of my hating
I hate and hate
Every**one**, every***thing.***
Don't think this makes my hate go away
It may even make me hate ***more***
But I love it in there
It's safe and I'm free
Hate is just great!
Please tell me
That you hate me.

THERAPY

Sometimes it feels like jail
And I am your prisoner
Sometimes it feels like a cradle
And I am your baby
Sometimes it feels like a kennel
And I am boarding here
Sometimes it feels like a hunt
And I am your prey
Sometimes it feels like the heavens
And I am your shining star
Sometimes it feels like dawn
And I am your sun
Sometimes it feels like a graveyard
And I will be buried here forever

WELL

I've been sitting in this chair
Week after week
And I realize I've only got one question for you,
Really, just one:
When is someone going to goddamn love me?
WHEN IS SOMEONE GOING TO GODDAMN LOVE ME?
CAN YOU ANSWER ME THAT?
If you can't answer me that
Then this is all a goddamn waste of time
When is someone going to goddamn love me?
Well?

CACTUS

What's with that stupid little cactus on your desk?
It looks ridiculous…
I'll tell you, though,
Sometimes I feel like I'm a cactus
Trying to figure out how to live all these years
With no water
No rain
Hot in the big, empty desert
Poking out those sharp needles
So no one will touch me…
Look at how some of those needles
Have fallen off
Isn't that interesting?

COWGIRL

Did you always have that little cowboy on your shelf?
I never saw it before!
My grandfather used to buy me little cowboys
I would always ask for a cowgirl
But he said they didn't have them
So each time he visited
He'd bring me a new cowboy
And I'd line them up on my shelf
And I'd dream about being a cowboy
Even though I was a girl
Me, a cowboy, isn't that ridiculous?
I can't ride a horse
I hate the outdoors
And I'm a girl
How could you have that cowboy on your shelf
All these weeks
And I never noticed?

CHECK

There's 5 minutes left in the session
And I haven't told you
What I really wanted to tell you
What I really **needed** to tell you
It's probably too late now
It'll have to wait
And I'll have to be disgusted with myself
For the next week
For not having told you once again
And another minute just passed
And you're not going to make me tell you,
Are you?
And now it's time to go
Now where is my check?
I thought I had it right here…
What the hell did I do with my check?

AT THIS TIME

I've finally come to the conclusion
That no hug is ever going to be
Big enough for me
I've been looking for that hug forever
From my father
From my husband
From my kids
I believe I'm going to have to settle
I'm tired of wanting
What I'm never going to have
I think I'll go home after this session
And hug my kids
And hug my husband
Give what I can give
Take what I can get…
I don't think
I need to schedule a follow-up
At this time

THE WAY

You know that Beatles song,
"Happiness is a Warm Gun"?
Well, happiness for me is warm **blood**
Dripping down my leg after I've cut myself
I follow the stream down my thigh
Onto my calf
Trickling onto my foot
By then it's cooling off
And I stare at it as it dries
A thin red line
Showing me the way

SHAVE

I was the new kid
And stood under a tree at lunch
All by myself
Staring at another lonely girl
Noticing her hairy legs
And deciding, then and there,
That I'd start shaving mine
And that I suddenly knew what it was like
To be surrounded by people
And feel completely alone

HOURS

I would be embarrassed to tell you
How much time I take to get ready in the morning
But I will tell you, it's **hours**
I'm up at 4, 4:30
Dark as night outside
Shit—it **is** night!
My hair, my make-up
My clothes, everything
I stare at myself in the mirror
Hear my father go into his shower
Hear the newspaper
Land on the front step
Wonder who will be looking at me today
I really believe I will die
If no one is looking at me

REASONABLE

My plan was to go on a
Cross-country robbery spree
End up in California
Buy a boat with my money
And sail to this completely unpopulated island
That I read about
Just off the coast of Japan
Where I'd live and read and draw
All day
And it actually took me quite a while to
Establish the fact that
This was not a reasonable plan
I really hate that word:
Reasonable

WHAT I STEAL

A stuffed animal,
Newspapers, all the time
Cough syrup
A watch, which is stupid
Being that my father *sells* watches for a living
A bra
Sodas left and right
Gum, of course
Doesn't everyone steal gum?
A bottle of perfume
That broke in my pocket
I was sure the guard would smell me
On my way out
Onions, once
I'm not really sure why…
Onions…

SHOW

My parents keep asking me if I'm having sex
I keep saying, no, no,
But they just don't get it
I mean, sure, my boyfriend's shown it to me
He showed it to me,
And I was, like,
"Okay, so *now* what?
So *now* what do you want me to do?"

PMS

I was so relieved to learn
That guys get PMS too
Because that would explain
Why my boyfriend's
Been such an ass recently

COMPLAINT

My boyfriend had open-heart surgery
And now he's fine
But I'm not allowed to complain
About **anything** anymore
He doesn't want to hear it
"After what **I've** been through…"
He always starts
And then I'm supposed to shut up
Here's **my** question—
What good's having a boyfriend
If you can't complain to him?

SUCKS

My old boyfriend's getting chemo and radiation for a brain tumor
He has to use a walker to get around
'Cause the tumor's messing with his vision
I wish that he'd look normal again
I just wish that he'd look normal again
Try to imagine the biggest number you can imagine
And then make it even bigger
And that's how awful he looks
I brought him a McFlurry when I went to see him last night
Because I know how much he likes them
He looked up and took it without smiling
And then he just stirred it and stirred it
Staring into it
Wouldn't even suck
At the straw

BALD

Last year I was bald
I shaved my head
Because some guy I was sleeping with
Gave me head lice
Have you ever tried to get head lice
Out of dreadlocks?
And everyone made fun of me
They called me terrible names
But now I've got a new boyfriend
And he cut his long hair
To get a better job
And all I do is taunt him
For looking like a retard
I tease him all the time
Once until he hit me
I had it coming

STOPPED

I was making out with my girlfriend
We were really going at it
And then she pulled away,
Pushed me away,
And said,
"I have something to tell you...I'm gay."
We said nothing for the longest while
And then I pulled her close to me
And began kissing her again
But it didn't feel the same
I put my hand down her shirt
But it didn't feel the same
I didn't know what to do
Nothing felt the same
I was just stroking her breast
While she watched me
She wasn't moving or moaning or anything
My hand just kept stroking her
Until it stopped.

UNCERTAINTY PRINCIPLE

My girlfriend,
I can't tell if she wants me
Or doesn't want me,
Or only wants me
Because nobody else wants **her**
It's like the Uncertainty Principle
Is she a wave or a particle?
I guess I'll never know
But I keep trying to figure it out
Hit her with my electron beams:
My girlfriend's a wave
My girlfriend's a particle
Or maybe she's neither
Or maybe she's both

THE ANSWER

I don't know what's worse…
If I fall in love with a girl
Or if a girl falls in love with me…
If I fall in love with a girl
It's bad news
Because all I think about is her
Nothing gets done
I want her when I'm awake
I want her in my dreams
But if a girl falls in love with me
I'm a mess
I feel like I can't bear it
I will never successfully shoulder
The weight of her love
I'll see it in her eyes
And it will make me queasy
She'll smile at me
And I'll smile back
But it'll be a smile
That pales in the face of her radiance
I want to be worthy of that love
But I don't think I am
So I shrink in its face…
I think
I've answered
My own question

ACCUSE

My boyfriend accused me
Of having sex with his best friend, Ryan
When I didn't
All we did was make out.
And I was angry that he didn't trust me,
Didn't believe me,
So then I went and had sex with Ryan anyway
At least now I don't have to deal with being accused
Of something I didn't do

BEAT

We were outside
And my girlfriend laid her head on my chest
And she said she could hear my heart beating
She'd tell me when it would get fast
And when it would get slow
When it was fast and when it was slow
And I could feel it, too
And I realized it was the first time
That I knew that my heart was beating
And with her head on my chest
It just beat and beat
Fast and slow
And I was lying there
Not believing that
I'd never felt it before

WHAT I SAY BETWEEN KISSES

You're my baby
Don't ever leave me
I'll never leave you
You're mine forever
Oh, baby

REALIZATION

Nothing that I've ever done
Is as full of consequences
As a kiss

INSTEAD

I was too scared to ask Cindy out
So she and I did drugs all night, instead

ALL THE TIME

I'm angry all the time
Ever since my girlfriend got pregnant
Today, I pulled some guy out of the hallway
By the sleeve
Said, *"Follow me,"*
Shoved him into the bathroom
And told him if he ever looked
At my girlfriend again
I'd split his fucking head open
So he'd better apologize now
And he did
"I'm sorry, man, I'm sorry,"
He said,
"I'm sorry, man, I'm sorry,"
Over and over,
And I stood there watching him grovel
And it felt so good,
Really, it did.

BABY

My girlfriend's gonna keep the baby
And I think I'm gonna die
I see no reason to go on
My life is over
My mom says I better go to college
So I can make the child support payments
Child support at 17—
Can you **believe** it?
I say, why bother?
My girlfriend's gonna keep the baby
And I think I'm gonna die

TEEN FATHER

I was rocking my daughter to sleep
Last night
Watching her eyes grow heavy
Picturing the first boy
Who makes her cry
How I'll mangle him good.
Real good.

EXPECTANT FATHER

I'm so possessive of my girlfriend
Ever since she got pregnant
I'm just waiting for some guy
To put a move on her
So that I can beat his face in
I've been carrying all this anger
Since I was 11
I'd beat his face
Into a gray pulp

LISTEN TO ME

I get fatter every week
Just look at this balloon!
It's so taut, now, like a drum
Last night I was lying in bed
Just drumming away
Gettin' that baby to dance in there
Pounding a beat
On this bongo of a belly
Be bop boo bop
Rum tittee tum tum
My womb's a big drum
And listen to me,
Poundin' out the rhythm of life
Bum biddee bum bump
Bum biddee bum bump
Bum biddee bum bump

I DON'T KNOW WHY

I open my legs
And I let him

BRIGHT

Promise after promise
I made to myself
Oh, the me I would be
If I'd make good on
Even half of them...
My girlfriend in my arms
Parked in front of her house at night,
Singing her all the songs I was writing,
Everything dark, dark as could be,
But things seemed so bright,
So bright

COULD I REALLY HAVE BEEN THAT HAPPY?

Sixteen years old
Saturday nights in an endless winter
On the cold floor
Of my girlfriend's living room
Kissing and kissing and kissing
Kissing and kissing and kissing
Oh, Lord, did we kiss
This was before the hope
Had emptied out of my heart
This is the place
I must go back to

THE SEXIEST MOMENT IN MY LIFE

Was when she stood
Talking to me in the gym
The strobe lights flashing
Some horrible band
Mauling Led Zeppelin
Surrounded by our fellow
Seventh graders
And she asked me
"Do you know how they spell 'Led'
In Led Zeppelin?"
And I did
And she began taking off her necklace
For some reason
And I thought
I was going to faint
I thought
I was going to burst
With longing

THE WAY OF ALL FLESH

I spent the entire summer
After ninth grade
Masturbating to the cover of
The Way of All Flesh
This lurid woman under a street lamp
Oh, those breasts of hers,
How they'd tumble towards me
As I tear off her blouse
And fill my hungry hands

SWEET AND SOUR

The summer before my senior year of high school
I got major into yogurts
I couldn't believe how good they were
I'd be eating four or five a day
All different flavors,
Cherry, peach, blueberry
I'd stir up all that good fruit on the bottom
Watch the colors blend into the creamy white
And spoon it down
One after another
Something about the sweetness
And that sour taste
Seemed just right that summer
The summer before
It all changed

AMERICAN PIE

I heard
"Bye, Bye Miss American Pie" the other day
Pushing the cart down the aisle of the supermarket
God, do I have memories of that song!
Getting stoned in the parking lot after school
Discussing the lyrics
Who was The Joker? Who was Jack?
Who was the widowed bride?
We'd talk for hours about it
I know now I was lost then
But I didn't quite know it then
That was the beautiful part
You just didn't know you were lost
And you had all the time in the world
It took a few years till you figured that out
And of course by then it's too late
To do anything about it
No more time
And that's the day
The music really dies

DREAMING OF THE FIRE

I spent my entire third grade year
Dreaming of the fire
That would engulf the school
So that I'd have the chance
To rescue Jenna Phipps
Carry her out of the burning school
In my arms
Set her down safely
Under the jungle gym
And kiss her soft forehead
Until she awoke with gratitude
Threw her arms around me
While everyone and everything else
Just burned and burned
And burned away

NEVER WILL BE

Doris B., Doris B.,
All the boys knew Doris B.
She was the one who'd go all the way,
They'd whisper.
For a science fair project on "Word Association"
Her name showed up over and over
When the stimulus was "sex"
I'd watch her in the hallway
In between classes in junior high
Only a year older than me
But worlds and worlds away
High heels and purple eyeliner
I was prim and proper, no make-up
No easy lay
And while I knew I was better than her
While I knew I'd never be called "slut" and "tramp"
And, worst of all, "whore",
I was secretly jealous of Doris B.
Jealous of every slutty inch of her
From her bleached hair
Down to her painted toes
I'd lie in bed at night
Imagine I was screwing
All those horny ninth-grade boys
The ones I saw watching her
In a way I knew I was not being watched
In a way I knew I wanted to be watched
In a way I knew I'd never be watched
And never was
And never will be

STARTS

Here are some of the letters I tried to write to my first girlfriend:

Dear Kelly, I have been meaning to write to you for a long time...

Dear Kelly, You won't believe what I am about to say...

Dear Kelly, Do you remember me?

Dear Kelly, I know this comes out of the blue, but...

Dear Kelly, If only I could have written this letter 30 years ago...

Dear Kelly, I am sitting alone in a restaurant in a hotel in Cleveland...

Dear Kelly, This letter may be a mistake...

Dear Kelly, How are you?

Dear Kelly, If you are reading this, after seeing the return address, then I am already hopeful

Dear Kelly, Where to begin?

Dear Kelly, What comes to mind when you think of a blue Buick?

Dear Kelly, I hope this letter finds you doing well

Dear Kelly...

I WOULD LIKE TO TELL YOU

Once I thought I'd killed my baby
She just wouldn't stop crying
Oh, God, she wouldn't stop
Hour after hour
Wailing and shrieking
'Til I was
Wailing and shrieking right along with her
Who was louder?
I don't know
She screamed at me
I screamed at her
I screamed at God
Finally I just slapped her
Hard on her little, bald head
I would like to tell you
That I felt horrible
But I didn't
It felt really, really good
Especially because she shut up for a moment
It felt so good
I wanted to do it again
Better than screaming at her
I actually thought
A nice slap
Well, she stayed quiet
And that's when I thought
That she had died
That I had killed her
But then it started up again
I would like to tell you
That I was relieved
To hear her start up again

To hear her cries
But I really wasn't
That's how far gone I was
So I gave up
Stopped screaming
Stopped slapping
Just let her cry
Wishing I was dead

BAD BABY

My toddler
She was thwacking her baby doll
On the kitchen table
The other night
Just thwacking her
Over and over again
Saying,
"**Bad** baby, **bad** baby!"
I watched in amazement
How does she already know?

CHANGE

The first time I changed my son's diaper
Had him on his back
All belly, sausage limbs
And big head
And that tiny penis
Pointing at me
Aiming at me...

CRASH

We flew to Florida for vacation
My two-year-old son
Cried from the moment we got into the airport
Through the entire flight
Halfway there I looked down at him
His face caked with tears, snot, dirt, and candy
I was so sick of everyone's stares and comments
And his wails and sobs
I prayed for one thing
And one thing only
Let this plane crash
Please, God, just let this plane crash.

LOT'S WIFE

Sometimes I head out for work in the morning
And the house is like Sodom and Gomorrah
I'm leaving bedlam behind—
Fire and brimstone!
Dishes in the sink
Shoes untied
Homework scattered about
My husband yelling and screaming at the kids
Waffles burning in the toaster
I drive as fast I can
My foot to the floor
Like I'm never
Turning back

PAYBACK

This one's my payback child
She's paying me back
'Cause I drove my mom crazy
Some moms say,
"What did I do to deserve this child?"
Well, not me—I **know** what **I** did—
I made my mom nuts
And now this one's making **me** nuts
Meanwhile, my mom's gotta be laughing at me
Up in heaven
Laughing at her daughter's ass getting kicked
By her darling little **grand**-daughter
Hell, they're **both** probably laughing.
I wish I could hear my mom laugh.

LOOK

My son's become my mother
I see her
In the look he gives me when I speak to him,
The look that says,
"You are so full of shit
You are a worthless piece of shit."
My mother didn't have to say a word
For me to know what she was thinking
How the hell did she figure out
How to give my son
Her eyes?

STRANGER

My daughter strolled by
Grabbed my index finger
And shoved it into
Her belly-button
To feel all the lint.
She giggled,
But I didn't…
In my head I saw
My childhood hand
Being hijacked
Sent somewhere it didn't want to go
And when, after forever,
It was finally returned to me
It hung from my arm
Like a stranger
That I didn't want to know

LAP

My daughter was sitting on my lap
And then she asked me if I ever sat on *my* mom's lap
I told her I couldn't remember
And then she asked me if my mom loved me
I told her I wasn't sure
And then she said, *"Well, I love you,*
You're the best mom in the world!"
I don't know why I'm crying.

PRAYER

My daughter
May be the only female I know
Completely in love with her own beauty
It's not that she's all that pretty
Her hair is ragged, her complexion pocked
And, like every mother,
I wish she'd lose some weight
But I marvel at the prancing in front of her father
The careful mixing and matching of outfits
The satisfied nod in the mirror
As she finishes her hair…
Must she lose it like we all do?
Is it too late for *me* to be taught?
Her Facebook page is filled with selfies
Each with a bigger smile
Than the one before
She sends them to everyone she knows
I pray that what she doesn't know
Won't hurt her

HANDCUFFED

The school called me to say
That my son was being arrested
For having beaten a kid up.
I dropped everything
To get there in time to watch them
Walk him through the halls in handcuffs
And when they bent him down into the squad car
And pushed him into the back seat,
You know, it was like he had beat *me* up,
Not some kid

BOY CRAZY

Those posters of guys on my daughter's wall,
Well, if a boy is walking down the street
And sees them through her window
He'll know she's boy-crazy
He'll think he can have his way with her
So I made her remove them
And, you know, she was crying
When she tore them down
Just crying and crying
Like she was tearing down her soul
Or something,
Like she was tearing down her soul

LUNCH

My daughter wants me to take her out to lunch:
Why don't we go out for lunch together? she asks sweetly,
This is after treating me like shit for four days running,
Like shit, I tell you,
Bitching and moaning about her miserable life,
Refusing to help me, her room's a mess,
Complaint after complaint,
And I want to say,
I'll take you out to lunch, honey,
Sure I will,
But first I'm going to kill you.
Now isn't that ridiculous
To want to kill her
And to know that afterwards
I would still want to take her out to lunch?

DISCLOSURE

...And when my daughter finally told me
What the guy had done
I moaned and moaned
And I circled around her chair
While she sat and sobbed
And then I suddenly grabbed her face
Her wet cheeks in my hands
And my heart was crumbling
And all I could say was,
"It'll never...
It'll never...
It'll never happen again."

WINGS

Since the divorce
It's like my children
Are flying through the air
Catapulted from mom's house
To my house
Back to mom's
Back to mine
They land
Empty out backpacks, bookbags,
Roost for a few days
Then, *Fling!*
They're back in the air again
Soaring back to mom's
Sometimes I wish I could give them wings
So they could take flight
Fly anywhere they wanted to
Fly away from all this
Sometimes
I just wish I could give them wings

SHOT

I've got a copy of this e-mail
My son sent to a male porn star
He posed as a girl
And said he was a big fan
And wanted some nude pictures…
I'll be honest
I'm a homophobe…
I'm not ashamed to admit it
I don't buy any of this gay stuff
So if there's a shot for my son
To make sure he turns out straight
Then please shoot him

MY GAY SON

He always shovels my walk after snowstorms
He always helps me cook for holiday dinners
His partner always sends me the nicest thank-you notes
He always picks me up my favorite coffee
And grinds the beans himself
He always calls me on my dead husband's birthday
And on our anniversary date
My gay son does all these things
But when he leaves
I shut the door behind him
Wait until his car is out of the driveway
And then I lean against the door
So sad

LOVE

My 19 year old retarded son
Sitting once again
In his own shit
Not even asking me to clean it up
Although I will
And I do
Could I love him
Any less than I do
And still love him?

GOD IN THE HEAD

My dad has too much God in the head
The only thing he talks about is
God and the end of the world,
And, now and then, hell.
I'll tell you,
Sometimes I feel like I'm really *living* in hell
And then I'm so angry with myself
For even believing in hell in the first place
What the hell,
Maybe he's right
Maybe I need more God in *my* head
It's not like *I've* got all the answers
All I've got is bruised wings
I feel like an angel with bruised wings
Bruised from trying to beat my way out of hell
Into heaven
Beating against those gates that won't open
God damn it, this is hard.

LOVE CHILD

When I was 16
My father sat me down and told me
That he had another daughter
A daughter he'd never met
Who lives with her mother in Sonoma
"I made a mistake when I was 18,"
He said, solemnly
"And I've never forgiven myself"
I always think about my half-sister
Living out in California, almost 30 now,
Without her father, the father who is mine
Tall and thin, no doubt
Prettier than me, and blonde
And I think about my father
At 18,
I mean, I'm 18 now!
My father as a young stud
Making it with some drunk girl
In the backseat of his car,
On a deserted beach,
In my grandparents' basement,
Who knows?
And then hearing the words:
"Hal, I'm pregnant."
And his dropped heart,
And all of the empty years
My daddy's got a love child
And I don't think it's me.

HUNG UP

My dad left me when I was five
"I love you," he told me,
"I'll be back"
But he never was
I'd hear from him every now and then
By phone
"How's my pumpkin?"
But I'd hang the phone up
Try to avoid Mom's glare
Ever since then,
The funny thing is,
Whenever I'm rushing into the house
Because I hear the phone ringing
And I dash over to pick it up
And no one's there
And it's dead
I'm sure that's him calling
Asking how his pumpkin's doing
I stand there,
I can't quite hang up

I KNOW I SAID I WISH YOU WERE DEAD

I've never figured out if
I told my father I wished he were dead
On the day that he died
We were fighting all the time
My mom would always say,
"You're going to give your father a heart attack!"
...or would she?
Maybe I'm just making that part up,
It's all blurry
But I know I said, **"I wish you were dead."**
To him at least once
I just don't know if it was on the day that he died
He was a heart attack waiting to happen, anyway,
Drinking and smoking and a big beer-belly
We'd just scream at each other
He'd tell me he hoped I'd get drafted
So the Army would make a man out of me
Can you believe it?!
A father wanting his son to go to Vietnam?!
They were coming back in **pieces**
And he wanted **me** to go!
He probably wished **I** were dead more than I wished **he** were dead!
But he was dead before I was drafted
And the asthma got me out, anyway
So I'm still here
And he's not
Do you think I killed him?

LONG GONE

A kid I went to junior high with, Carl,
Lived right around the corner
Went nuts one year
Long hair, drugs, jail
The whole nine yards
One day, walking home from school
Probably a year or two after he'd been sent away
I found a notebook with his name on it
On the side of the road
I decided to drop it off at his house
Knowing he was long gone
But wanting to see what would happen
I rang the doorbell
A stern man
White shirt, thin tie, crewcut,
Answered the door
"I think this is Carl's," I said,
Handing it over to him
He took it
Narrowed his eyes at me
Trying to figure out what I wanted, I guess,
Then he just shut the door on me
Not another word…
I've got two kids now
One's going into middle school
I wonder if I'll be Carl's dad one day
Holding a phantom notebook
My son long gone

LEGACY

My dad,
He was always
Reading me the Riot Act
"I'm gonna have to read you the Riot Act!"
He'd yell
What the hell is a Riot Act anyway?
I still don't know
All I know is that
He was always ready to read it to me
Can't believe
I've never figured it out

CLAM

My father always referred to himself
And the rest of us
As *"happy as a goddamn clam"*.
Now since our family was a disaster area
From top to bottom
And since I know that clams cannot be particularly happy
Sitting at the bottom of the ocean
Unable to move
Or think
Or feel
I now understand that
Telling everyone that we were all
Happy as a goddamn clam
Was about right

OVER

I finally told my father I was gay
And he was quiet for a while
Then he said,
"Don't worry, I love you, I love you,
"Don't worry, I love you, I love you,"
Over and over again
But I could tell that with every
"I love you" he was really saying
"Don't worry, you're going to hell,
Don't worry, you're going to hell,"
Over and over again.

IDIOT

My father told me that what I said was idiotic
And when I told him I didn't think so
He said, ***"Well, then that makes you an idiot"***
And I thought about that for a while
And, you know,
After thinking and thinking,
I realized that I was an idiot
For thinking about it

WHAT I WAS THINKING ABOUT

My father,
A stinking drunk,
Was killed by a wrecking ball,
Pounded him right in the head,
He probably didn't even know what hit him
I still remember going with my mom
To identify him at the morgue
13 years old
Putting my hand behind his skull
When no one was looking
It was so soft,
Like jello,
Or pudding,
Or tapioca,
Desserts, is what I was thinking about,
Just desserts

MY FATHER'S PRAYER

My father was in Bergen-Belsen
He told me that one day
They lined up a bunch of prisoners,
Single-file,
One behind the other,
Pressed them tightly together
To see how many could be killed by a single bullet
I'll always think of my father standing there
Praying for the fat and the bones
Of the poor men in front of him
The poor men who saved his life

BIRTH

My niece complained that it was
Twenty minutes before she got to hold her baby
Twenty minutes while they took him to the NICU
To check him out
She was crying about those twenty minutes for two whole days,
Twenty minutes without my baby, she sobbed
As she held him to her chest
I wonder if she knows what it's like
To go about twenty *months*
Before you hold your baby
Twenty months
While your baby's in foster homes
And an orphanage
And you wait and wait
Hungry to hold him

PLEA

I tell my mother
Over and over
I'm not having sex with my boyfriend
My birth mother had sex at sixteen
And that made me.
Does she think I want to get pregnant,
Have a baby,
And then give it away
Like my birth mother gave *me* away?
What, does she think I'm stupid or something?

AGAIN

I want my parents to adopt again
So that the baby can sleep in my bed
So that I can remember what it's like

DUE

When you're adopted
You're always waiting to be shipped out
I know my parents are thinking that
They're thinking every day
How much better their life would be
Without me
Sometimes I feel like I'm a big, cardboard box
They'll pick me up one day
Address me to the orphanage
And just leave me next to the mailbox
Postage due

GRAND

It's going to be all right,
Mom told us that night,
I'm leaving but I'll be close by,
And Daddy loves you,
Daddy loves you, too
I've just gotta get out
I'm going crazy
It'll be better once I've gone.
What a grand smile my mom had
When she was lying

5:00

About an hour before my father came home
My mother would put on her make-up
Make a big drink,
Belt it down,
And sit in the living room,
Leafing through a magazine,
Waiting…
Me, I'd go upstairs to my room and hide
No matter what the season,
It always seemed dark when he came home
Every goddamn day felt like winter

ASHAMED

I was always ashamed of my grandmother
She'd pick me up after school
Outside the building, on the sidewalk
All the other kids rushing to their
Normal looking parent and grandparents
And there's my quiet grandmother
In her kimono
Never smiling
Tinier than everyone
I wouldn't even acknowledge her
Walked yards in front of her
So as not to be associated with her
As if I wasn't already associated with her
The only Japanese kid in my class
She'd silently trail me
I'd say nothing to her
She'd say nothing to me
Until we got to the house
I was always so ashamed of my little grandmother
Now I'm ashamed I was ashamed

DARK NIGHTS

That was the year
My mother finally took to drink
My retarded brother had to be institutionalized
Another one of my father's companies failed
And her mother died of cancer
I didn't blame her
Gin and tonics from morning till night
"Another one, sweetie,"
She'd request
Clinking the ice in her glass from her chair
I was only too happy to help
Little bartender, I,
Ten years old
And proudly delivering
It wasn't too bad, really,
She was a pleasant drunk
Always happy to have me home
Except for the nights,
The dark nights, I'd call them,
When she'd hate me
And swear at me,
And wing her glass at me
Say the nastiest,
Most horrible things
I wish I were my brother,
I'd think
Hiding in the basement
With the cats
While she hollered for me
Calling me names

REVELATION

I grew up in a converted farmhouse
And one time, for a change,
Took the back stairs up
To my parents' bedroom
And all I remember
Is the moonlight moving
On my mother's butt.

BROTHERS

I was watching the clouds yesterday
And, oddly enough,
Thought of my brother
Big, billowy
Blocking out the sun
Leaving me in the shadows
Or is it the shade?

WRONG

Do you want to know what it's like
To admit you're wrong in my family?
Just take a knife, slice your wrist,
Then dunk it in a pool of sharks
And feel them coming after you
Just feel the teeth tearing your flesh
Until all you feel is tooth on bone
And then what you feel is nothing

NUTS

My sister and I were emptying groceries
From my brother's beat-up station wagon
You have to have someone hold the hatch up on this car
Or else it'll slam down on your head
So my sister says,
"You get the bags, I'll hold the hatch,"
So I'm leaning in to get the bags
And the hatch slams down on my head
Almost knocked me back into the trunk
"What the hell are you doing?" I yelled.
"Sorry, I was reaching for my cigarette," she said.
I'll tell you,
The only way to grow in my family
Is to grow nuts

LIST

We were in the grocery store
And my mother had to go to the bathroom
So she asked me to get started with the shopping
And to cross things off the list as I picked them up
And I told her I don't need to do that
I shop with*out* a list
But she said just *do* it anyway
So I did
And then she came back from the bathroom
And started picking out apples
And I told her I already got the apples
Look, I've even crossed them off the list
But she didn't care
She threw the apples in the cart anyway
She's angry no matter what I do

JUST THE SAME

"I love you and your sister just the same,"
My mother always said
So how come once we were shopping
And I saw a dress I liked
And she said it wasn't for me, too grown up,
And later that week
My little sister comes prancing out of her room
Wearing that dress?

SLICE

My mom always burns the steaks on the grill
So I sliced off my own piece before she got to it
And put it in the oven to cook it by itself
So my mom finds out of course
And just goes nuts
Screaming and hollering about my not being a team player
Yelling at me for not thinking of anyone but myself
And meanwhile my piece of steak is sitting in the oven
Getting cooked and cooked
Until it was time to eat
And I couldn't eat

JELLO

My mother-in-law was baby-sitting for my daughter
And fed her Jello:
Lime Jello!
She fed my daughter Jello
We're strict vegetarians
We don't kill **anything**!
And she fed my daughter Jello!
Jello's made with pigs' knuckles!
I can't believe my poor baby had to digest pigs' knuckles!
Doesn't she know that there's vegetarian Jello?
You can get it anywhere!
Any flavor!
How could she do this?
I feel so bad for my baby
I told my mother-in-law
Never again!
If she feeds her Jello again
She'll **never** babysit, **ever**!
Lime jello with pigs' knuckles
I could kill her.

ALMOST NOBODY

I told my parents I was bi
And they were like
You can't be bi
You're either gay or straight
But you're not bi
Almost nobody's bi
So I told them,
Well, then, I guess
I'm almost nobody

HERE'S WHAT I WANTED TO SAY

We left the party
It was snowing
Snowing so thick
You could barely see
And I wanted to say to him:
I love you no more
I just love you no more
It's true, you're right,
I love you no more
But it was too hard to see
My husband was straining to see
The car was all over the road
We skidded once
But he regained control
We got home
And once again
I said nothing

HERE'S HOW I DECIDED TO LEAVE MY HUSBAND OF 18 YEARS

I had my car in the shop
And the guy said I needed new brakes
How much will that cost? I asked
I couldn't believe his answer
It was a breathtaking amount!
Do I really need to do it? I asked
Well, he said,
I sure wouldn't let <u>my</u> wife drive a car
With brakes that look like this.
Those were words I did not know
Husbands ever said

DEER

My husband says nothing anymore
Every conversation is like pulling teeth
Won't talk about his work, about the kids
About our not having had sex in months
Nothing
          God,
Did I tell you
The car in front of me hit a deer the other night?
There was this giant explosion in the dark
And my windshield was suddenly covered with tufts of fur
Couldn't see at all for a few terrifying seconds
Until it all blew away
I drove past
The deer was on its side
On the side of the road
It had these giant, empty eyes

HOW, EXACTLY

How, exactly,
Did it happen
That I married this man,
That we speak but don't talk
That we screw but don't love
That we touch with no warmth?
I remember him when we met
So handsome and scared
And I gave myself over to him
Over and over, I gave myself over,
And now it's like I've gone under
I don't understand
He wants me every night
Like a panting dog
I'm like a sad bone
A sad, sad bone
That never breaks
That's gonna break

SHOULD HAVE KNOWN

We were on our honeymoon
A Caribbean resort
And my husband wanted
A romantic picture of us
We asked a guy working on the beach
But he fussed and fussed with the camera
Couldn't figure it out, for some reason
My ex got fed up
Grabbed the camera from the poor guy
Sent him on his way
And just took pictures of me standing by myself
With the sun setting
Never developed

SEQUENCE

My husband left his iPhone out
So I was just looking through the photos he'd saved
And found one of him at a luncheon
Sitting next to the woman he works with
She looked so pretty
He looked so happy
I went so nuts

WHAT I'M THINKING ABOUT

Every time I have sex
I think that it's the last time I'll have sex
That I could die the next day…
Will I die awake or in my sleep?
Will it be by illness or accident?
That's what I'm thinking about
When I have sex
It seems to summon ghosts
Tells me that
Time does not appear to be on my side

COMMERCIAL

Does anyone else
Think of television commercials
While they're making love?
My wife and I were doing it the other night
And what was going through my head?
"Stays crunchy, even in milk."

STUD

I had this reputation in college
For being a stud
For giving girls multiple orgasms
It was like they'd line up
Outside my dorm room each weekend
Anticipating something
Boy, the pressure was on!
But I did what I had to do
Seemed to work fine
Until I married one of those girls
Now there's no magic
She never comes,
She's sure to report each time,
It's not the same,
She complains,
Why isn't it the same?
She pleads,
Turning away, crying,
I ask you, now,
Why isn't it the same?

SINGLE SOUL

Some nights I park outside my lover's house
And secretly watch him going about his business
With his wife and kids
He says his wife's not very bright, not very caring
But I can't tell from watching her
He says his two sons are very musical
But I never see them practice
There's a dog in there, too,
I watch her trot from window to window
She's probably the only one who knows I'm there
But *she's* not talking…
Anyway,
One night I watched him and his wife
Sitting in the living room
Having what looked like a serious talk
Of course, I assumed they were talking about me
She had finally discovered the affair
By careful study of his cellphone bills,
Or, better, he was finally telling her that he'd met
The woman of his dreams
Pretty, smart, *fabulous* in bed
So much happier with me than with her
But then they suddenly stood up
Stood up and kissed!
And they shut the lights and headed upstairs
And those lights went out, too
I sat in the car for a while
Then drove home
But had to stop and get gas
I was empty
All by myself at the station

11:30 at night
Not a soul around
Dark
And not a single soul

CLOUDS

The whole flight home
The morning after
I screwed up
And screwed around
With that woman at the hotel
I just stared down into the clouds
Thinking about my wife
Getting the kids off to school
Scraping the ice off the car
Driving to work
And I'm there in mid-air
Guilty as hell
Wishing I could just push out the window
Dive down into those clouds
And sink forever

WHAT IS WITH ME

Falling in love with every one
Of our babysitters?
I drive them home after my wife and I return
And it's like I'm driving them home from a date
Struggling for questions they can answer
SAT's, boyfriends, rock bands
I steal glances at their soft silhouettes
Imagine their long hair in my fingers
Then they hop out of the car
With their cheerful thanks
I watch their fathers,
Not a whole lot older than me,
Let them in and wave me away
I drive home so lonely in the dark
Listening to the songs on the radio
Pull up to my house
Just sit in the driveway with the engine off
For a long time
Listening
Not going in

THE WORST PART

Oh, he loved me, I **know** that
I mean, he started playing music again
Once we started seeing each other!
He said that he hadn't played the violin for years
And now he was playing all the time
He'd bring it over
And after we made love
He'd take it out of his case
Playing Mozart and Bach
And I'd lie there, naked in the warm sheets,
Feeling like he was playing me…
Did I think he'd really leave his wife?
Yes, of course I did!
I mean, he was playing the violin again
His wife couldn't care less about the violin,
He said,
How could he ever go back to the woman
Who had stopped his violin?
But you know what the worst part was?
The worst part wasn't him telling me
The worst part wasn't him picking up the violin
The worst part wasn't watching him drive away
Knowing I'd probably never see him again
The worst part was
That my mother was right
My mother
Who doesn't like music
Who never played an instrument
In her entire life

WHERE ELSE?

I met a woman the other night
In a bar—where else?
We drank and danced
It was so dark, she was so hot
The rain outside
Then she put her drink down
Looked at me,
Reached for my hand,
Said,
"I love you deeply
And will never remember your name."
Do you think I'll ever forget her?

BEEP-BOOP-BEEP

My phone is killing me
No room for thought
No chance to slow down
This woman and I have been trying
To end our affair for months
In the old days, I could
Count on a busy signal,
It took a while to dial,
For god's sake
Now it's *beep-boop-beep*
Speed dial, there we are
Call waiting
Never a busy signal
She can always reach me
I can always reach her
At work, at home, in the car,
Christ, even the shower,
Beep-boop-beep
There I am telling her to love me
There I am an hour later
Telling her not to call
I'm done with her
There I am another hour later:
"I need you, I need you."
I tell you,
My phone is killing me

ENOUGH

To get back at my wife
For having had an affair
I bring it up at very awkward times
We'll be in the car with another couple
Driving home from dinner,
And I'll say,
Out of the blue,
"But why did you have to sleep with him?"
She never answers
She just shakes her head
Of course there's the awkward silence in the car…
She used to ask me not to do this anymore,
"How long are you going to embarrass me? _Forever?_"
She'd plead with me
But now she doesn't even plead
She's resigned herself to the humiliation
Small price to pay, I guess she figures,
For all that pleasure,
I wonder when she'll have had enough
I wonder when I'll have had enough

ALL THESE YEARS

And I never knew
That my wife
Kept something under her pillow
Every night
Since we were married.
How is it that I did not know?
How could she keep a ribbon there
And never tell me?
Now every night
I carefully slide my hand under her pillow
And stroke it
Thinking about her
Feeling the weight of her head
Feeling the weight of her past

EYES

I watch my son with his girlfriend
I see he can't take his eyes off of her
I remember my husband looking at me like that
The lightest toss of my hair
Just the act of unbuttoning my coat
Made him look so hungry
God, I loved it
When he couldn't take his eyes off of me

DOWN

My husband, he'd be nothing without me
He'd fall into a weeping heap
But he doesn't know this,
He thinks *I'm* the weak one,
I'm the needy one,
He just can't see how empty his life would be
Without me
I'm gonna show him, though,
I'm gonna give him the lesson he'll never forget
I promise you that
And he will go down, I tell you,
He will go down

THE BREAKUP

Her love for me feels like an iron
Pressing down on me, removing my wrinkles
Her love for me feels like ice
Freezing cold, making me hard
Her love for me feels like a broom
Sweeping me out of her way
Her love for me feels like a cricket
Chirping, chirping, gobbled by lizards
Her love for me feels like a foot
A foot pressing down on my neck
Until I can't breathe
And don't want to breathe
Breathless
But I've gotta breathe

THIS MAY NOT BE WHAT YOU NORMALLY HEAR

But I am very happy with the divorce proceedings
Thus far
I love having my lawyer deal with my husband
Don't have to listen to his shit anymore
I love keeping a list of everything that happens
How often he screws up visits
How many times he sends the kids home
In dirty clothes, unfed
I love thinking of him in his little crappy ass apartment
Little loveshack with his little whore
Paying out 800 dollars a month rent
When he's always been so tight with a buck
I rub my hands with glee
When he calls the house
My house, now
And the kids don't want to talk to him
You must think I'm a nasty woman
You must think I'm a terrible mom
I don't care what you think, really,
I am having a ***ball*** of a divorce
Sit in judgment of me, if you want,
You're a guy,
Sit there feeling sorry for my husband
Thinking, ***"What a bitch—no wonder he had an affair."***
You can think what you want
Me, I'm going to enjoy the hell out of this divorce
Every stinking second of it

EVIL

My wife left me, my wife left me
She's telling everyone that I'm evil
That I'm an evil monster
That I turned my son against her
But I didn't turn him against her
I want him to love his mom
I want him to see his mom
But he doesn't want to see her
"Dad," he says,
"Mom frightens me,
Mom frightens me when she hears the voices,
Mom frightens me when she talks to ghosts."
She sent letters to all our best friends
My mother, even, my sisters,
Telling them I was evil
A letter explaining all the evil things I've done
I saw the letter
Someone showed me one
Filled with obscene drawings of me
It's lies, all lies
But who're they gonna believe
Me or her?
Me, who didn't write a letter
Me, who lies in my empty bed each night
Unable to sleep
Hearing the word,
Hearing it:
Evil, Evil

BENCH

"I picture us old,
Sitting on a bench
Feeding pigeons,"
I told my wife,
Exhausted from another vicious fight
And she shocked me…
She smiled.

POTATOES

I don't want to be one of those couples
Sitting in a diner
Pushing potatoes around their plate
Saying, *"How are the potatoes?*
Do you like the potatoes?"

LONESOME

Last week
Was the first snowstorm
Without any kids at home
No wearing of pajamas inside out,
Praying for a snow day
No watching the late night Weather Channel
No listening to the early morning traffic report
Just the snow
My husband and I
The casserole we ate
The wine we shared
Quiet
And lonesome

LULLABY

The Percoset
It feels so good
It feels so good
It feels so good
The Percoset
It feels so good
How will I ever stop it?

MORE

They say the key to happiness
Is not having what you want
But wanting what you have
But I'll tell you
I want what I have
And I'm *still* not happy
Because I always want more of it
Have food, I want more food
Have love, I want more love
Have sex, I want more sex
Have sleep, I want more sleep
Have chocolate candy, I want more chocolate candy
Sometimes I lie awake at night
And cry in my bed
And feel like I just need more tears
More and more tears

NOVEL

I figured I needed to get drunk
To start my novel
So I got a fifth of vodka
Poured the whole thing into a pitcher of Kool-Aid
Cherry
And started writing away
And it worked!
Here's what I've got…
The story of a girl
Whose father raped her
And now she's an adult
She's remembering everything that happened
And she goes in search of her past
In search of her father
But the funny thing is
He really didn't rape her
Or did he?
I haven't figured that part out yet
I've gotta get more vodka and Kool-Aid
So I can find out

FEATHERS

I've slept with 25 guys this year
I make sure I lose control
By drinking myself into a stupor
Shot after shot
Oh, the guys love me
They wait for my weave and stagger
My slurred words
That's when I know I'm ready
I'm on my back in no time
Thinking about fathers floating down…
Did I say fathers?
I meant feathers…
Thinking about feathers floating down
I always think about feathers

WHISKEY

Sometimes the whiskey whispers to me
And I drink it
Sometimes the whiskey shouts at me
And I drink it
Sometimes the whiskey cries for me
And I drink it
Sometimes the whiskey is shy
And I drink it
Sometimes the whiskey is whiskey
And I drink it

IN RETURN

My girlfriends and I
We'd ask these guys
To get us beer
They must have been
Thirty years old or something
We got the beer
But we didn't realize
That they wanted something
In return
But we still wanted the beer

BOYS AND BOOZE

I was overweight as a kid,
"A big girl", they would say,
Until I got into boys and booze…
Boys and booze
And that's how I finally lost it

DRUGS OF CHOICE

Vodka and semen
These are my drugs of choice
Each night I drown in one or the other
Sometimes both
Like last night
I was with a big man
Large and careless
Wild and dirty
Oh, you don't want to know
Let's just say
I'm all sore today
Vodka and semen
You know I'll leave here
And drink again
Can't you stop me?
I'm still so sore
Can't you stop me?

HANGOVER

Waking up is the worst
A moment of horror
Then the light attacking me
Like a jackhammer to the skull
Every sound
A pencil jabbing in my ear
My son at my side,
"Mommy, Mommy,
Look what I found!
See what I did!"
Oh, sweetie, I can't look,
I can't see,
Go away, go away,
Go away

RECOVERY

Tomorrow
I am determined
In spite of the evidence
To get out of bed
To make myself coffee
To drink the coffee
I don't have to **enjoy** the coffee
Just drink the goddamn coffee
To rinse the cup in the sink
To put the wet cup
In the rack to dry
To sit back down
Look out the window
Watch the trees
And think about coffee
Only about coffee

SOBER

I decided it was finally time to stop drinking
I **meant** it this time
So I promised myself one last good bottle of Scotch
I drove back to my old neighborhood
Went into the liquor store
Where I stole my first beer, back when I was 12,
Bought the best single malt I could find
And started drinking it
Right out of the bottle
Walking up the streets
Where I grew up
Past my house, past my grandparents' house,
Past the houses of all my aunts and uncles
Drinking and drinking
Getting stoned and stoned
And when I was finally finished
Do you know where I was?
Right in front of my old piano teacher's house!
I **loved** that man!
He **believed** in me!
I stood at the bottom of those old stone steps
With an empty bottle in my hand
Swaying, weaving,
My head spinning
And I started humming
Humming Mozart
Mozart that he taught me
Just a little boy on a big bench
Playing Mozart
For all the world to hear
Haven't had a drink since
Don't believe I will

GIVING UP

I brought my children
To my parents' gravesites the other day
They never knew their grandparents
Dead before they were born
They were running around
Like it was a playground or something
At first I was annoyed
"This is a cemetery!" I snapped at them
They quieted for a while, stood by me,
But then went back to playing hide-and-seek
Behind the headstones
I gave up and let them be
So, I told my mother,
These are your grandchildren.
So, I told my father,
These are your grandchildren.
God, you would've loved them.
I told the kids we should leave something behind
A balloon! They yelled
So we went driving around this dismal neighborhood
All run down
Until we found a party store
You know what they picked out?
A Ninja Turtle balloon!
For my parents!
Well, I gave up again
What the hell
We drove back to the cemetery
And I tied a Ninja Turtle balloon
To their headstone
I drove away crying and crying
Oh, God, did I cry

All the way
All the way home

ASHES

I was surprised my father's ashes
Were so coarse
I expected fine sand,
Bleached and white,
Like the beach he used to take me to
Instead it was this pebbly mixture
Brown and gray
Like a million tiny bones
Sifting through my fingers
Over and over again

FOR THE LIFE OF ME

Soon I will have to bury my father…
When I was a kid
I heard my father talking about having
To bury my grandfather
But I was little
And thought he said "Berry" my grandfather
I had this image of covering him up
With berries
All kinds,
Strawberries, blueberries, raspberries
From his feet to his head
Lots and lots of berries
For the life of me
I couldn't figure out
Why you would berry an old man
My father and I laugh at this story
I actually thought of bringing some berries to the hospital
When I went to visit him yesterday
You know, make light of it
I mean, **he** knows he's dying
He knows it's time
But it just didn't feel right
I guess I'm not ready
To berry my father

SOON

The other day
My father reported to me,
"I want to die soon."
Couple of heart attacks
Diabetes,
Asthma,
A stroke,
Can't walk, can't read,
Incontinent
He's had it
But I do wonder
Why he said, **Soon**
Why not, **Now?**
I suppose you're never quite ready
To say **Now** when it comes to
Your own death
"I want to die soon, honey,"
He said,
Taking my hand,
It was thin and shaking,
But still warm,
"Very soon."

RIDE

The train-ride home from college
After I'd learned that my father died
Took a few hours
But it felt like a month
And all I can remember
Is this black cloud in my head,
And the houses and the trees
And the houses and the trees

PATRIMONY

Once I **was** a son
Now I **have** a son
What's the word for who I am?
"Father" doesn't seem to work
Something's missing
Someone's missing

OH, TO SEE

My mother's face
It's been so long, now
Rises up like a breeze
And disappears as quickly
It's been so long, now,
Oh, to see my mother's face

I THINK I REMEMBER

My mother's foot
Pushing the cradle I rocked in
There was rain out the window
And she hummed and knit
I felt the rocking
I still feel the rocking
The rain and the cradle
My mother's foot

ALL THOSE POEMS

I see you write poems
I was reading your book in the waiting room
It made me think about my dad
He liked poetry
I remember him reading poems to us when we were little
I wonder if he ever wrote poems, too…
Like, did he ever write poems to my mom?
"I look into your eyes…"
Stuff like that?
It's strange to think about
They're both dead
I was 9 when my mom died
Diabetes, she left us all
My dad didn't marry again until I was 19
All those years without her
All those poems he never wrote

BEDPAN

My father
Lying there in the crumpled sheets
On his bedpan
Wanting to tell my mom about the affairs he had
"I want her to know so she can forgive me,"
He pleads
Not knowing or caring that it'll break her heart
Not knowing or caring that it's too late
Not knowing or caring that it's so selfish of him
To dump this last load on her
On top of all the other loads he's dumped on her
All these years
"I just want her to forgive me,"
He pleads
Could there be a bigger asshole?

MY DEAD FATHER

My dead father
Left us when I was a baby
I suppose because of this
I picture him more dead than alive
The bullet hole through his temple
On a rainy night
The blood spurting out
The police, the ambulance
The hospital staff
His spirit departing
The corpse in the coffin
Lowering him into the ground
All sealed away
That's how I think about my dad
A sealed coffin
In the silent mud

DIED A YOUNG MAN

My father spent a year
In bed one year
Crunching on large apples
Reading philosophy
Listening to Gershwin
"Died a young man,"
My father would say,
Shaking his head,
Whenever I came in after school
To say hello and sit with him
Gershwin's "Lullaby"
Would be playing
Over and over again
I still can hear
Those sad strings
When I lie in bed at night
Waiting to sleep
Missing him

NOW

My mother is dead now
Who can I blame?
My bitterness is now mine,
Not hers
My darkness is now mine,
Not hers
My sadness is now mine,
Not hers
What is going to happen now?
This is what I have always wanted…

MAKES ME WANT

Wherever I go now
I feel their eyes
And the inaudible words
He's the man who lost his son
He's the man who lost his son
They say it so that they don't have to feel it
They say it so that they don't have to know it
They say it so that it won't happen to them
A silent vaccine
They think they say it to themselves
But I hear it all
Oh, I hear it all
And it makes me want to kill
And it makes me want to cry

NEW YEAR'S EVE

Our son died back in August
On New Year's Eve
We got call after call
From friends and family
Wishing us a good year
Wishing us a better year
Fuck 'em all, and their good wishes
Not one of them was my son

STARING

Months after my daughter died
I don't know how many
I was in a restaurant
Across from two lesbians
With their adorable daughter.
Of course, I instantly hated them
For having a daughter
When I no longer did
I studied her like she was mine
Curly hair, chubby cheeks,
Not at all like my daughter
She had her mothers wrapped around her fingers
They were feeding her snacks
Giving her crayons
Three, maybe four years old
Completely in charge
I remember my daughter at that age
I remember the disasters at restaurants
The tantrums, the spilled drinks,
The embarrassment
I'd give anything to go back there now
One mother caught me staring
She kind of glared at me
As if I was staring at them because they were gay
I wasn't staring at them because they were gay
I'm not sure why I was staring at them
Maybe I was staring at them because if I stared long enough
I could be just like them

THESE ARE THE THINGS

The never-ending red light near my office
The itchy throat during allergy season
My wife's fake smile
The missing socks
The interrupted television show...
These are the things that bothered me
Before my son died

HOLD

Sunday was Picture Day at church
All the families showed up
Me, I showed up holding a picture of my son
I told the photographer
"Take the picture of me holding the picture of my son."
She paused for a second,
Then understood.
It turned out great
I was smiling
And of course my son was smiling
After all, it was a *picture* of him smiling
So now I've got a picture of me
Holding a picture of my son
On the mantelpiece at home.
Please hold me.

A LONG TIME

My husband came home with four large cans of shaving cream
On sale at Walmart!, he happily announced,
Two days later, he's dead of a heart attack
For weeks I've stared at the four cans
Which he left on the bathroom sink—
He never puts stuff away—
So last night I took the four cans
And emptied each one into the bathtub
Takes a long time
And then I took off my clothes
And sat in the tub
Filled with shaving cream
I didn't cry
I didn't weep
I didn't wail
I just sat there in the dark
In the shaving cream
Quiet, quiet,
Everything so quiet
In the foam
Then I stood up
Showered off
And watched all the white
Wash down the drain

LATE SUNDAY AFTERNOON

I spent the whole day with my wife in the hospital
She didn't budge the entire time
Didn't even open her eyes
I watched the sun rise over the buildings
And then start to fall
The baseball game began and ended
Another loss
As the sun set
I left and went to Target
Had to get something, I don't remember what
Sunday night, the store was empty and quiet
I'd never seen it that way
I stopped at the aisle of knives
Knife after knife after knife,
All gleaming…

AMAZED

I hate seeing my mom
Now that she doesn't recognize me
"Oh, hello,"
She says, kindly
In a voice that's not hers
What do you talk about
With someone who gave birth to you
But doesn't know you?
She'll forget it all anyway
I don't know why I wonder
So I make small talk
She asks me what I do for a living,
Am I comfortable?
She seems pleased to see me…
My mom used to yell at us kids
Something fierce
Same woman—***scream*** at us!
The whole neighborhood
Would know when my brothers and I were in trouble
I used to be so embarrassed
But now I wish she'd yell at me
Like she used to
I think that as I sit with her
Telling her about her grandchildren
Same stories I told her the week before
"Oh, I have grandchildren?"
She'll ask,
Always amazed
Maybe I envy her
What's it like to be always amazed?
To greet every piece of news with amazement?
I think that

As I sit with her
Hoping she'll amaze me
And say my name
Just say my name

HOPE

I remember going to the petting zoo
As a little girl
And stroking a deer's new horn
Warm to the touch!
Under all that hardness,
Blood

ALL THAT

My two Army buddies and I
Walk the mall each Friday morning
Up and down we go
Staring in the storefronts
We never really talk about The War
But it's like it's always there
All that we saw
All that we killed
All that…
The mall's empty when we walk
Starts filling up as we finish up,
Get our coffee,
And sit and watch
The mothers pushing the strollers
All the stores opening up
We just stare at each other and nod
We know what we were fighting for

FORGETTING TO BE HAPPY

They say you can't be happy until you learn to forget
Well, I guess that means I'm never gonna be happy
Ain't **no** way I'm gonna forget what's happened to me
And if I did
I'm not sure I'd want to be that kind of happy
Forgetting to be happy…
Man, that's fucked…

BLACK ICE

The other morning
I never saw it:
Black ice
Just touched the brakes
And I went flying sideways
Into oncoming traffic
Wheeling and turning
The horror movie
Slowly unreeling
The one you dread
But can't stop watching
Knowing what's going to happen
But not knowing how
Not knowing when

CASH

Just once I'd like a briefcase full of cash
Like in the movies
Where they open it up
And the camera moves in
And there's stacks and stacks of neat, crisp bills
Someone's hand flips through them
Like a deck of cards
God, that would be great!
I'd walk around all day
Telling myself,
"I've got a briefcase full of cash!"
I wouldn't even spend it
Just to know I had it
I'd carry it with me everywhere
No one suspecting
That this unsuspecting briefcase
Was making me rich
At night I'd go home
Lock the door
And count it over and over again
That's ***gotta*** be the life
A briefcase full of cash

ME

I'm always in love with somebody else
But never in love with me
Why is that?
Why can't I feel the same lust for myself
That I feel for others?
What a change that would be!
Instead of pursuing some guy
I'd pursue me
Instead of craving some guy
I'd crave me
Instead of dreaming of some guy
I'd dream about me
And hold me
And want me
And that would be very different

EMT

Nobody prays for things to disappear
Like I do
When I hear there's an accident
I flip on the lights and the siren
Floor it
But the whole time I'm praying
That everything will be gone
By the time I get there
No body parts
No screams
No blood
Just once I'd like to
Come upon the scene of an accident
And see nothing but
An undamaged guard rail
The cars gliding smoothly by
A few wild flowers
Swaying it the breeze
On the side of the road
Instead of DOA
I'd call it POA
Peace on Arrival

BIRD

Sometimes I stare at our little lovebird
And I feel like a little boy again
Caged

TABLECLOTH

My neighbor shakes her blue flowered tablecloth out
Every evening
I envy her down to my bones
Dinner with her husband and kids
A tablecloth full of delicious crumbs
The fluttering over her lovely deck
And the clean tablecloth draped back on her table
Ready for tomorrow's breakfast
Such order, such care
And me with my stupid, plastic placemats

THE MOON

On Monday
I saw the moon
At the museum
Well, it was the moon rocks
I couldn't believe
This dull, gray dirt
Was from the white, shining moon
I've stared at for 49 years
I've cried under that moon
Made love under that moon
Slept under that moon
Got married under that moon
And there it was
In a box:
The moon…
I was so upset
I went out that night
To look for it
Found the crescent
Smiling at me
Saying,
That wasn't me
That's not me
I am here for you, still,
The moon.

DIFFERENT

I chose the wrong college
I chose the wrong husband
I chose the wrong job
I chose the wrong house
I've got the wrong children
The only thing I choose correctly
Are my clothes
And my cigarettes
Everything else I screw up
How could this have become my life?
Oh, it all should have turned out different
It all should've been so different

SHORT STORIES

All my relationships are like short stories...
No matter how good they are,
They're over before you know it.
Why can't I have a novel
With a beginning,
A long, long middle
And an end that takes forever to get to?
Why can't I just have a big, boring novel?

SIX YEARS OLD

You know how I can tell I'm growing up?
I like to eat things I didn't used to like
I used to hate Kalamari, now I love it
I used to hate Shake and Bake
Now I tell my mom, ***"Make Shake and Bake!"***
I even eat pepperoni on my pizza now—
They used to make me gag!
I wonder what I'm going to want tomorrow?

HIM, ALL RIGHT

I had the same dream again
But this time the radio picked up signals
Instead of static
And I heard my father's voice for the first time
I could barely make it out
But it was him, alright
"Italy, Italy," he was saying,
"Italy, Italy."
I woke up chanting,
"Italy, Italy," to myself
"Italy, Italy."
I smelled dark coffee the whole day
Kept hearing arias
Saw the most beautiful sunset at night

MILK

I've been dreaming these days
About the children I never had
Last night they started off
As milk in a glass
I knocked it over
And suddenly there were kids
Spread out across the kitchen floor
"We are here! We are here!"
They shouted
Leaking all over the floor
I'll never be able to clean this up,
I thought,
It's all wet, now,
All wet,
I woke up weeping

FACE

I dreamt I made my own face
When I was in my mother's womb
I was like Mr. Potato Head
Found a nose, stuck it in the middle
Found two eyes, stuck them up top
Found two ears, stuck them on the side
My mouth and chin, stuck them on the bottom
Ugly, ugly, is how I looked
Still do
Couldn't my mother have helped?

THAT GUY

I dreamt I saw my birth mother last night
She was sitting at a table
Holding hands with some guy
And then she looked up
Knew it was me
And she dropped the guy's hand
Stood up
Started walking towards me
And I didn't know what to do
And then I woke up
It was the middle of the night
And I couldn't get back to sleep
My throat was all dry
All I could think about was
Who was that guy she was with?
Who the **hell** was that guy?

HAIR

I dreamt my mother
Had planted my hair
She seeded and watered my scalp
Until my hair began to grow
In long, long braids
Thick, like rope
Piling over my shoulders
Thick and heavy
Like a waterfall of hair
Longer and longer
Until it hit the ground
And started coiling around me
So I couldn't walk
So I couldn't move
I saw my mother on the other side of the room
It was raining
It was raining hair
And because of the hair
I couldn't reach her
To thank her
Or to choke her

FOG

I dreamt
I knocked at a door
Attached to no house
And it opened up
To a valley deep with fog
I stepped into the valley
Disappeared for a time
Then reappeared at another door
Attached to no house
I knocked
And it opened up
To a mountain covered with fog
I climbed the mountain
Arriving at another door
I knocked
And it opened up
To a bridge over a dark river
Spanning fog
I crossed the bridge
Arrived at another door
Attached to no house
I knocked
And it opened up
To a bear
Large and furry
Hidden by fog
It chased me down
Clawed me till I bled
This dream, I believe,
Is about
Fog

GOOD DOG

I had a dream in which
There was a terrible catastrophe
And I had to euthanize my dog
Because I couldn't save both her and myself
And my heart flooded with sorrow
But just as I was about to do it
My dog woke me up
With her wet nose
Looking at me with her big eyes, like,
"What were you <u>thinking?</u>"

ALL OVER

I had a dream
In which I realized
How much I wanted to be loved
But also how much I wanted *to* love
And I woke up
With an ache,
This ache all over,
Just wanting to die

DEMON

I had a dream that a demon was on top of me
Trying to strangle me
A demon that I could only see with my eyes closed,
When I opened them, it would disappear,
So I ran into the hall to tell my mom
And found her sitting in the living room,
Watching TV
And when I told her about it she said,
"Yeah, I've had that dream, too
You just have to tell the demon to get the hell out,
Then he won't bother you anymore"
She didn't look up from the TV.

BOAT

I dreamt
I was rowing a boat
Across the moonlit water
Rowing away from the old me
Rowing towards the new me
Dip and pull
Dip and pull
Looking up to see
That the moon wasn't moving
And neither was I

POINT OF ROCKS

I spend too much time wondering
Where I left my dream
As if I could go back and get it
I actually dreamt once
That I had rediscovered it
In the attic
Of an empty house
In a ghost town by the sea
Called Point of Rocks
I rejoiced
Then started to cry
Does it still count
If you find your dream
In a dream?
I hope so
Because usually
My dream is nowhere to be found
I looked up Point of Rocks
On an atlas once
Actually found it
Less than an hour
From where I live!
Weird, huh?
Point of Rocks
So nearby
I should go there
But I probably won't.

WIND

I dreamt
I was so lonely
That even the wind forgot about me
The wind!
How lonely are you
When the wind forgets about you?
It blew and blew all night
Blew right by me
Up to the stars
Then back again
Blew the waves in from the ocean
Until I was drowning in the sea
Praying, ***"Wind, wind,***
Don't you see me?
Won't you lift me?"

MOURN

Why do I mourn
What I lose in dreams,
The things I never even had?
I wake up and everything I own
Is in my room
In the same place
But I spend the day
Thinking about the wings I had at night
The golden wings that carried me
Across the hills

MONTHS

I have met with you for months, now
I have dreamt I was sand
I have dreamt I was a thief
I have dreamt I was a frog
I have dreamt I was a blood vessel
That leaked
And could not carry any blood
I have had all these dreams
And nothing has turned out as I had hoped

CONFESSION

If I tell you my dream
What is left of me?
If I tell you my dream
You'll know
If I tell you my dream
I'll hate myself
(By the way,
If I *don't* tell you my dream,
I'll hate myself, too)
If I tell you my dream
I'll have to kill you
I will, you know,
I'll kill you

FISH

I dreamt that we had our session at the beach
And you cut off all my fingers
Threw them into the sea
And they became fish
Beautiful, colorful fish
Swimming around
And I dove into the water
Trying to catch the fish
But they couldn't be caught
I was gasping for air
Gulping water
The lovely fish darting by me
While you stood on the sand
Watching me
Calmly cleaning my blood from your knife

BUT ME

I had a dream
I heard the music
No one's ever heard
It was strange music,
Beautiful music
I could sing it for you
But I won't
It must remain the music
No one's ever heard
But me

SONG 1

I dreamt I was singing my heart out
It flew out of my throat like a bird
Carrying my song away with it
Red and beating
It soared into the heavens
Red wings flapping
I was all ears as I listened
For my song
But could not hear it
Something of importance has left me

SONG 2

I dreamt I awoke
To a beautiful song
That I could not sing
It went,
Where am I going?
How will I get there?

EPILOGUE

WHAT IT TAKES TO BE A THERAPIST

To nod your head
In the face of unutterable pain
And to say,
Yes, yes,
I hear you,
Yes.